DELAY was first produced by Amanda Fawcett
in a co-production with Bristol Old Vic.

DELAY

by Timothy X Atack

DELAY was first performed at the Bristol Old Vic,
Bristol, on 19 June 2025.

DELAY
by Timothy X Atack

CAST

LIN	Jyuddah Jaymes
The Voice of SILAS	Alex Lawther
The Voice of AUTO	Vera Chok

CREATIVE TEAM

Writer, Composer and Sound Designer	Timothy X Atack
Director	Tanuja Amarasuriya
Set and Costume Designer	Bronia Housman
Lighting Designer	Alex Fernandes
Movement Director	Laïla Diallo
Casting Director	Amy Ball CDG
Production Manager	Jo Woodcock
Research and Evaluation Consultant	Dr Hassan Hussain
Voice Consultant	Carol Fairlamb
Assistant Director	Lau Batty
Costume Supervisor	Rhi Good
Company Stage Manager	Kay Hudson
Producer	Amanda Fawcett
Assistant Producer	Bilqees Khalid
Music performed by	Timothy X Atack and Shamira Turner
Image Designer	Malcolm Reid
Photography by	Paul Blakemore

June/July 2025 production supported using public funding by Arts Council England

CAST

Jyuddah Jaymes | LIN

Jyuddah Jaymes is a British actor and graduate of Bristol Old Vic Theatre School. His recent performance as AJ in Tarell Alvin McCraney's *Choir Boy* (Dir. Nancy Medina, Bristol Old Vic) marked a celebrated return to his training ground, earning widespread critical acclaim and contributing to the production's three Black British Theatre Awards in 2024, including Best Play and Best Director.

Jaymes made his professional stage debut in *Twelfth Night* (Dir. Kwame Kwei-Armah, Young Vic), followed by *The American Clock* (Dir. Rachel Chavkin, The Old Vic), and *Romeo and Juliet* (Dir. Rebecca Frecknall, Almeida Theatre), where he played Tybalt.

Jaymes broke into screen with his debut role as Aubrey in season two of *Clique* (BBC), followed on by *Sanditon* (ITV), where he portrayed the much loved Otis Molyneux. His recent work includes *Django* (Sky/Canal+), hit-action movie *Fight or Flight* and Mike Leigh's latest film *Hard Truths*. Other notable credits: Jesse Owens in *The Boys in the Boat* (Dir. George Clooney, MGM); *Criminal* (Netflix) and *Hijack* (Apple TV+).

He has recently finished filming *The End of It* for Elation Pictures/BBC Film and will be seen alongside Will Sharpe and Paul Bettany in the new series adaptation of *Amadeus* for Sky Studios later this year.

Alex Lawther | The Voice of SILAS

Alex Lawther has just wrapped *Leonard and Hungry Paul* for BBC/RTÉ, playing Leonard, and will next be seen in a lead role in the new FX/Disney+ series *Alien: Earth*, directed by Noah Hawley, released this summer.

On stage, Alex began his work as an actor in David Hare's *South Downs* in 2011 on the West End – his work since includes playing the title role in Robert Icke's *Hamlet* in New York; the late Peter Brook's *The Tempest Project* at Les Bouffes du Nord, Paris; Stephen Daldry's *The Jungle* at the Young Vic, on the West End and St. Ann's Warehouse in New York; and Tim Crouch's *An Oak Tree* at the Young Vic.

He is perhaps best known for his role in the BAFTA & Peabody Award-winning Channel 4/Netflix series *The End of the F*cking World*. He can also be seen in the Disney+ series *Andor* opposite Diego Luna, as well leading a critically acclaimed episode of *Black Mirror: Shut Up and Dance*.

Most recently, Alex starred opposite *Titane* star Agathe Rousselle in *A Second Life*, which premieres at Tribeca 2025. Other screen work includes Ridley Scott's *The Last Duel* and Kenneth Lonergan's BBC/Starz adaptation of E.M. Forster's *Howard's End*. In his first film role Lawther portrayed the young Alan Turing in the Academy Award-winning feature *The Imitation Game*, for which he won the 2014 London Film Critics' Circle Award for Young British Performer of the Year.

As a writer-director Alex made his directorial debut with the 2023 short film *For people in trouble*, a love story set in a time of collapse, starring Emma D'Arcy and Archie Madekwe. It premiered at Tribeca Film Festival 2023 and was nominated for a London Film Critic's Circle Award. His second short film, *Rhoda*, premiered at the London Film Festival in 2024. He is currently developing his debut feature.

Vera Chok | The Voice of AUTO

Vera Chok (them/they) is an actor, writer, and performance maker.

Theatre includes: *2:22 A Ghost Story* (UK tour); *Burnt at the Stake* (Shakespeare's Globe); *The Winter's Tale* and *Harlequinade* (Garrick Theatre); *Chimerica* (Almeida and West End transfer); *The Hard Problem* and *World of Extreme Happiness* (National Theatre); *Twelfth Night* (Regent's Park Open Air Theatre); *L'Etranger* (The Print Room); and *The Paper Man* (European tour).

Vera was most recently on TV as series regular Honour Chen-Williams, head of the first ever East Asian family in a UK continuing drama in Channel 4's flagship drama, *Hollyoaks*.

Further screen credits include: *Chimerica*, *Chewing Gum* (Channel 4); *Cobra* and *Fortitude 3* (Sky). Vera also played the lead in the multiple award-winning feature film, *Dream Agency* (Forest Fringe).

CREATIVE TEAM

Timothy X Atack | Writer, Composer and Sound Designer

Timothy X Atack is a writer and composer working in stage, screen, audio, and books. His writing for stage and performance includes: *Heartworm* (winner of the Bruntwood Prize for Playwriting 2017); *Babel's Cupid* (Runner-up, Yale Drama Series 2020); *Ocean Confessions* (Sura Medura, Sri Lanka); *Dark Land Light House* (MAYK/Bristol Old Vic); *Supernova* (Mayfest); *The Bullet and the Bass Trombone* (MAYK/Bristol Old Vic/UK tour); *The Morpeth Carol* (Bristol Old Vic); *M32 is Also a Galaxy* (Paines Plough/Bristol Old Vic); *The Freelance Magdalene* (Bristol Old Vic); *Buzzard* (Theatre Bristol/Bristol Old Vic) and *Astronaut* (Arnolfini/UK tour).

Writing and directing for screen includes the short film *All My Dreams on VHS* (Audience Award, NexT Bucharest 2009). Writing for audio includes the BBC productions *Vidya Wade*, *Beethoven Can Hear You*, *The Beard*, *Forest 404* (WGGB Best Radio Drama 2020, Radio Academy ARIA Best Fictional Storytelling 2020), *The Stroma Sessions* (Afonica, nominated for the Tinniswood Prize 2017), *Phonophone*, and *The Morpeth Carol* (Radio Academy Award Best Drama 2014). He is also a regular writer of *Doctor Who* audio dramas for Big Finish Productions.

As a composer, musician and sound designer he has worked with Angel Tech, North Sea Navigator, Neil Bartlett, Raucous, Selina Thompson, Nik Partridge, Edgar Wright, Bodies in Flight, Nikesh Shukla, Lucy Cassidy, Matt Lucas, Tobacco Factory Theatres, Manchester Royal Exchange, Bristol Old Vic, Channel 4, BBC Radio, We The Curious, and English Heritage among many others.

He is a resident at Pervasive Media Studio, Watershed, a writer on attachment at National Theatre Studio 2023–24, and co-founder of the multi-artform company Sleepdogs alongside Tanuja Amarasuriya.

Tanuja Amarasuriya | Director

Tanuja Amarasuriya is a director, dramaturg and occasional sound artist, working in theatre and related forms. She won the 2024 RTST Sir Peter Hall Director Award.

As director, her work includes: *Out of Sorts* (Theatre503); *The Paper Man* (Improbable/Tobacco Factory/Soho Theatre); *Ocean Confessions* (Sura Medura, Sri Lanka); *Dark Land Light House* (MAYK/Bristol Old Vic); *The Bullet and the Bass Trombone* (MAYK/Bristol Old Vic/UK tour); *Check the Label* (Bristol Old Vic); *The Morpeth Carol* (Bristol Old Vic); *M32 is Also a Galaxy* (Paines Plough/Bristol Old Vic); *Astronaut* (Arnolfini/UK tour); *Julius Caesar* (Malcolm X Centre/Bristol Old Vic Theatre School); *We Anchor in Hope* (LAMDA Linbury Studio); *Absolute Scenes* (The Marble Factory/Bristol Old Vic Theatre School) and a forthcoming new production of Noël Coward's *Private Lives* (Bolton Octagon/Mercury Theatre/Rose Theatre/Northern Stage).

She was associate director with Dominic Cooke on *Good* (Harold Pinter Theatre), *Medea* (@sohoplace theatre), and *Rock Follies* (Chichester Festival), and was the National Theatre's staff director on Max Webster's production of *The Importance of Being Earnest*. As dramaturg or sound artist, her work includes projects with Kaleider, Raucous, Selina Thompson, Channel4 Random Acts, Nancy Medina, Chris Thorpe, and Luca Rutherford. She is a resident at Watershed's Pervasive Media Studio, and co-founder of the multi-artform company Sleepdogs alongside Timothy X Atack.

Bronia Housman | Set and Costume Designer

Bronia Housman has been designing sets and costumes for theatre, opera, dance and pop music performances since 2003. She trained on the Motley Theatre Design Course. She is currently the Head of Design at Bristol Old Vic Theatre School.

Recent design includes: *Sleeping Beauty* (Oxford Playhouse); *Pinocchio*, *Mumsy* (Hull Truck); *The Borrowers*, *Remarkable Invisible* (Theatre by the Lake, Keswick); *Ground* and *PoliNations* (Trigger); *Jane Eyre* (Stephen Joseph Theatre); *The Wizard of Oz* (Salisbury Playhouse); *Table*, *The Kitchen Sink* (New Vic, Newcastle-Under-Lyme); *Hedda* (Bristol Old Vic); *The Rubenstein Kiss*, *Amy's View*, *After Miss Julie* (Nottingham Playhouse); *Strange Blooms* (Shobana Jeyasingh Dance); *Imago* (Glyndebourne); *The Rodin Project* (Sadler's Wells and touring).

Bronia was associate designer with Es Devlin for over ten years, working on the closing ceremony of the 2012 Olympic Games, many stadium pop music shows, numerous operas around the world plus plays for the Royal Court, Complicité and the Donmar Warehouse.

Alex Fernandes | Lighting Designer

Alex Fernandes is a lighting designer for contemporary performance, and was the recipient of the 2013 Michael Northen Bursary. Selected lighting work includes *DOMESTICA* (Battersea Arts Centre, UK and international tour); *Swimming Pools* (Teatro de la Abadia, Spanish tour); *Double Double Act* (Unicorn); *Système AI* (Sadler's Wells); *Minor Planets* (HAU Berlin); *Kim Kardashian* (Balé da Cidade de Palmas, Brazil); *Heartbreaking Final* (Wiener Festwochen & Centre Pompidou); *Two Billion Beats* (Orange Tree); *Paradise Now!* (Bush Theatre); *L'Addition* (Avignon International Festival/international tour); *A View from the Bridge* (Headlong); *The Beginning* (Staatstheater Mainz, international tour); *Ghosts of the Near Future* (Barbican); *Die Glasmenagerie* (Theater Basel); *Scenes from a Repatriation* (Royal Court). He was the technical director of Forest Fringe between 2013 and 2016, and is the current Touring Technical Manager for Forced Entertainment.

Laïla Diallo | Movement Director

Laïla Diallo is a Canadian-born, Bristol-based performer, movement director and choreographer.

Movement direction/choreography credits include: *The Man Who Planted Trees* (Company Six-0); *The Snowy Day* (Can't Sit Still/Polka Theatre); *Arch* (Kaleider); *The Winter's Tale*, *Oliver Twist* (Tobacco Factory Theatres); *ABBA Voyage* live band choreography; *The Pearl Fishers*, *Rigoletto*, *Otello*, *Un Ballo in Maschera* (Opera North); *War and Peace*, *Aïda* (Canadian Opera Company); *Emilia*, *Three Seagulls* (Bristol Old Vic Theatre School); *Wonder Boy*, *Nutcracker* (Bristol Old Vic); *Capriccio* (Garsington); *Thérèse Raquin*, *All's Well That Ends Well* (National Theatre); *The Prince of Homburg*, *Dance of Death* (Donmar Warehouse); *Tis Pity She's a Whore* (West Yorkshire Playhouse); *Days of Significance* (RSC/Tricycle).

Amy Ball | Casting Director

Amy Ball is an award-winning casting director working across theatre and film, with a strong focus on new writing and contemporary performance. From 2007 to 2021, she was Head of Casting at the Royal Court Theatre, where she was responsible for casting over 30 main-stage productions, including *The Glow*, *Is God Is*, *The Cane*, *Pity*, *X*, *Anatomy of a Suicide*, *Cyprus Avenue*, and *The Ferryman*. Many of these productions went on to have acclaimed West End and international runs, including *Hangmen* (Wyndham's/Atlantic Theatre Company), *The Ferryman* (Gielgud/Bernard B. Jacobs Theatre), and *Jerusalem* (Apollo Theatre).

Her recent theatre credits include *Medea* (Fictionhouse/@sohoplace); *Drive Your Plow Over the Bones of the Dead* (Complicité/Bristol Old Vic/Barbican); *Good* (Harold Pinter Theatre); *The Hills of California* (Neal Street Productions/Sonia Friedman Productions, Harold Pinter Theatre); *Cold War*, *Portia Coughlan* (Almeida Theatre); *Nachtland* (Young Vic); *Slave Play* (Noël Coward Theatre) and *The Pillowman* (Duke of York's Theatre). Amy has also cast productions such as *Rosmersholm* (Duke of York's Theatre); *hang* (Royal Court Theatre); *Jumpy* (Royal Court Theatre/Duke of York's Theatre); *Girls & Boys* (Royal Court Theatre/Minetta Lane Theatre, New York); and *Killology* (Royal Court Theatre/Sherman Theatre).

In film, her credits include *Ballywalter* (2022), *The Unlikely Pilgrimage of Harold Fry* (2023), and *In Camera* (2023), with upcoming projects in development with Film4, BBC Film, and emerging independent directors. Amy is also a strong advocate for early-career filmmakers and regularly collaborates on short and independent film projects.

Jo Woodcock | Production Manager

Jo Woodcock is a Bristol-based production manager and event coordinator.

Recent credits include: *Bakkhai, Boudica, Angels in America, Cherry Orchard, Darknet* (Tobacco Factory/Bristol School of Acting); *Sleeping Beauty, Hurry Up Father Christmas* (Oxford Playhouse); *Elevate Festival, Play Back* Audio Drama Project (Theatre Royal Bath); *Forest of Dean Fringe Festival* (Wyldwood Arts) *Revealed, Oz* (Tobacco Factory); *cheeky little brown* (Bristol Old Vic/tiata fahodzi); *Same Storm Same Sky* (Bristol Old Vic/Many Minds); *Art of Resistance* (Trinity Community Arts).

Jo was Production Manager of Travelling Light for over 20 years, touring award-winning productions for children and young people to venues, schools and community spaces all over the world. Prior to this she stage managed for a variety of companies, including the Royal Court, The Crucible Sheffield, Bristol Old Vic, Birmingham Rep, Leicester Haymarket, Show of Strength and Circomedia.

In addition to her production management work, Jo stage manages the Cabaret tent at Glastonbury, coordinates events for Marmalade Trust Charity and is guest stage management tutor for the University of Bristol Drama Department.

Dr Hassan Hussain | Research and Evaluation Consultant

Hassan is a writer, researcher, and facilitator. Having recently completed a PhD investigating the de/construction of gay men in contemporary British theatre, his practice explores the transformative effects of (queer) histories and lived experiences on present and future iterations of (queer) identities, communities, and (sub)cultures.

As a proud Birmingham Bab, Hassan is particularly invested in situating his work within the city and has secured development funding from Arts Council England to redress the underrepresentation of queer South Asian voices in British playwriting and is currently working on his first full-length play. Moreover, his involvement in coordinating and producing a diverse array of (research) panels around queer identity, creative workshops, festivals, and live-art events further enriches his practice. Hassan is keen to be involved in projects that centre queer experiences, performances and histories.

Carol Fairlamb | Voice Consultant

Carol Fairlamb has been a voice coach for thirty years. Trained at the Royal Central School of Speech and Drama, she spent a decade as Head of Voice at Bristol Old Vic Theatre School.

Productions for Bristol Old Vic Theatre include: *Touching the Void, A Good House, Reverberation, Wonder Boy, The Little Mermaid*. Other productions include: *Blackbird, Love-lies-bleeding, A Midsummer Night's Dream, Tales of Vienna Woods, Don's Party* (Sydney Theatre Company); *Riflemind* (Sydney Theatre Company and Trafalgar Studios); *Romeo and Juliet, Twelfth Night,*

A Midsummer Night's Dream (Regent's Park Open Air Theatre); *Touching the Void* (Duke of York's Theatre/Parco Theatre, Tokyo); *Dr Semmelweiss* (Harold Pinter Theatre); *War Horse* (National Theatre tour).

Lau Batty | Assistant Director

Lau Batty is a writer, director and creative facilitator based in Bristol. She has assisted Jesse Jones, Kirstie Davis, Nancy Medina, Alix Harris and Jay Zorenti-Nakhid and worked with the Royal & Derngate, Simple8, The Minack Theatre, Bristol School of Acting, Beyond Face and Tobacco Factory Theatres. As a writer and deviser she has worked with Lightbox Theatre and New International Encounter.

This year, as an Associate Artist with Beyond Face she is developing her play *How to Grieve Correctly in a Tuvaluan Household with Other Oceanic References*. Her work focuses on celebrating her Pasifika heritage and exploring indigenous knowledge systems and their solutions to systemic injustice.

As a creative facilitator she works with young people and communities who experience barriers to accessing the arts, throughout the South West. She works as a creative facilitator with Threefold Theatre and has previously worked with Unique Voice, Bath Theatre Academy, PAPER Arts and Prime Theatre.

Rhi Good | Costume Supervisor

Rhi Good is a Bristol-based costume supervisor and maker. Since graduating from Bristol Old Vic Theatre School in 2020, she has worked predominantly in theatre and performance, and as a commissions based maker.

Her supervision credits include: *Boudica*, *Bakkhai*, *Double Bill: The Britz/Codetta*, *Angels in America*, *Elsinore*, *Revealed* and an upcoming production of *Crucib*tch* (Tobacco Factory); *The King's Speech* (Watermill Theatre); *Princess Smartypants*, (Watermill Theatre/tour); *The Ugly Duckling*, *A Christmas Carol* (Irving Studio Theatre); *The Meaning of Zong* (Bristol Old Vic).

As a costume maker, her work includes: *CinderElla* (Royal Tenbury Wells); *Aladdin* (Cheltenham Everyman); *Wonder Boy* (Bristol Old Vic); *Fools Delight Circus* (Ham Court); *House of Flamenka* (Peacock Theatre); *Mother Goose* (Cheltenham Everyman); *Cinderella* (Belgrade Theatre); *The Marlowe Sessions* (Malthouse Theatre); *Dr Semmelweis* (Bristol Old Vic).

Kay Hudson | Company Stage Manager

Kay is a theatre and events company stage manager and a TV production coordinator.

Theatre credits include: *Hamilton* (UK and Ireland tour); *The Curious Case of Benjamin Button* (Southwark Playhouse); *If You Fall* (Bristol Old Vic); *Revealed* (Tobacco Factory Theatres); *A Level Playing Field* (Jermyn Street Theatre); *Dick Whittington*, *Puss in Boots*, *Mother Goose*, *Cinderella* (Hackney Empire Theatre).

Events credits include: 51st UAE National Day Celebration, 2022 Commonwealth Games Opening and Closing Ceremonies, 2015 Liberation International Music

Festival, 2014 Commonwealth Games Team Welcome Ceremonies, charity events in Parliament, Buckingham Palace and St James's Palace.

TV credits include: *Election Night* (BBC); *Amol Rajan Interviews*, *The One Show*, *Crimewatch Live*, *The Secret Lives of Animals*, *Dogs in the Wild* (BBC Studios); *The London 2012 Olympic and Paralympic Games* (Olympic Broadcasting Services).

Amanda Fawcett | Producer

Amanda Fawcett runs Amanda Fawcett Productions Ltd and is Company Producer at Firebird Theatre. Previously, she was Programme Producer at HOME, Manchester where she produced and programmed theatre, performance, music and dance and curated festivals. Amanda was Lead Producer on HOME's co-production of *The House with Chicken Legs* (Olivier Award nominee for Best Family Show – 2024), working closely with co-producers Les Enfants Terribles. Amanda was Associate Producer at China Plate, lead-producing a midscale tour of Inspector Sands' critically acclaimed *Wuthering Heights* (named in The Stage's Top 50 shows of 2023). She's produced, collaborated and toured work with organisations across the UK and internationally, including: the National Theatre, New Diorama, The Rose Theatre, Oxford Playhouse, Royal & Derngate Northampton, China Plate, Many Minds, Dibby Theatre, Bristol Old Vic, MAYK/Mayfest, Lost & Gone, Raucous, Les Enfants Terribles and Breach Theatre. Amanda was a Stage One Supported Producer (Autumn 2024 cohort).

Bilqees Khalid | Assistant Producer

Bilqees Khalid is an actor, emerging producer, and director. She holds a BA (Hons) in Acting from Bath Spa University. Following her training, she began developing her skills in producing, with a strong interest in collaborative, community-focused work.

As a Participation Assistant at The Egg, Bilqees has supported a range of programmes for young people, schools, and community groups, contributing to workshops, performances, and outreach projects.

She is passionate about storytelling that centres queer and global majority voices; work that challenges dominant narratives and creates space for joy, nuance, and identity. As a creative, she is particularly excited by projects that move beyond trauma and instead celebrate the richness and complexity of underrepresented experiences.

Amanda Fawcett Productions Ltd

Amanda Fawcett Productions Ltd exists to support creative processes with care and ambition and produce bold and brilliant new work. The company is proud to have launched the 'Proper Job Programme' alongside *DELAY*. 'Proper job' references the pressure that marginalised folks often feel from parents/family to get a 'proper job' outside the arts. The team behind *DELAY*, want to show other underrepresented creatives that we belong in the industry and deserve sustainability, career progression and visibility in high-profile theatres. Supported by Arts Council England.

Bristol Old Vic

Bristol Old Vic is the UK's longest continuously running theatre and has welcomed millions of people through its doors since opening nearly 260 years ago.

Led by Executive Director Charlotte Geeves and Artistic Director Nancy Medina, and with investment from Arts Council England, the organisation is committed to platforming and creating opportunities for the multitude of stories that Bristol and the UK have to offer.

Bristol Old Vic offers a year-round programme of inspiring, original new work. Alongside the co-production of Timothy X Atack's *DELAY*, recent productions include Flora Wilson Brown's *The Beautiful Future is Coming* (which transfers to the Traverse for summer 2025), the premiere of Amy Jephta's *A Good House* in partnership with the Royal Court, the European premiere of Matthew López's *Reverberation*, Nkenna Akunna's *cheeky little brown* with tiata fahodzi, and the new musical *Starter for Ten* which returns to Bristol in autumn 2025. It also has one of UK theatre's biggest learning and engagement programmes; and has recently relaunched its artist development programme, including a five-year commitment to new writing which includes working with writer, Winsome Pinnock. Plus, through Bristol Old Vic On Screen, audiences across the world have seen its productions live or on demand.

'We will make a theatre which is for our whole community. Not a passive place, but one of activism. Not one voice, but many. We will ask questions of ourselves and of Bristol. We invite you to come on in and help us make this building sing with possibility.' – *Nancy Medina, Artistic Director*

bristololdvic.org.uk

Acknowledgements

The team behind *DELAY* would like to thank Bristol Old Vic staff for their support, Layla Barron, Ali de Souza, Kenan Vurgun, Israel Bloodgood, Adam Gent, National Theatre Studio, Watershed, Maddie Hindes and the team at Nick Hern Books, the Independent Theatre Council and Stage One.

DELAY

Timothy X Atack

People

LIN, *on stage, male, an astronaut, and Silas's lover*
SILAS, *voice-over, male, an author, and Lin's lover*
AUTO, *voice-over, a system-announcement software*

Action

Occurs forty years into the future, on board the *Oshūn*, a one-man spacecraft on a pioneering mission to Nova, a distant world, a planet intended as humanity's first extraterrestrial colony.

Lin is the *Oshūn*'s sole human occupant.

Auto is a distinctly artificial voice, without a distinct personality. Silas is only heard via audio messages from Earth.

The *Oshūn*'s environment has circadian artificial daylight, which brightens and dims depending on the 'time of day' and has tinctures for sunrise and sunset.

NB In this text, any description of Lin's actions during the playback of Silas's messages has been kept deliberately minimal, to allow for full discovery by performer and director.

Note on Text

In the stage action, an ellipsis (…) indicates a kind of punctuation in the flow, perhaps a pause, perhaps a thought, perhaps a beat. It shouldn't be taken as gospel.

This text went to press before the end of rehearsals and so may differ slightly from the play as performed.

Scene One: The Stars Unspinning

Day 304, 16:00.

The observation chamber.

Mechanical sounds and a rumble of processed air, ticking over...

...and fading.

In the observation chamber: LIN *is floating in zero gravity.*

He is occupied by huge and troubling thoughts...

...and attempting to distract himself by watching the implacable, distant stars.

Scene Two: Lin is Alive

Day 304, 16:20.

The comms centre.

The gravity here is normal.

LIN *is at the communications terminal.*

LIN. I'm awake. It's day three hundred and four out here and I'm –

(*Annoyed at himself.*) Stop recording. Do not send.

An 'end recording' chime.

AUTO. Recording stopped.

LIN. Do not send.

AUTO. Message unsent.

LIN. Delete message.

AUTO. Message deleted.

LIN *thinks*.

LIN. Record.

'Recording' chime.

I'm awake, I'm alive. Everything's real and I love you.

…

I've started and deleted this – must be ten, fifteen times, so hopefully I'm running out of ways to be stupid about it.

What did we say? Honesty within the rules.

(*Deep breath.*) My biggest fear was I'd come out of the freezer and I'd have forgotten your face. They told me during training they still don't know what the freezer does to the brain. People have been known to come out of it with different accents –

I don't think my accent's different? But then I wouldn't know. If it *is*… changed, then… Silas, please, when you reply…

Don't tell me if I'm sounding… alien to you, I couldn't…

(*Happier.*) But I didn't forget your face! Cos soon as I woke, I went to personal storage, and looked at your photo, and it matches, my memory's the same –

Sudden self-doubt –

But what if I've forgotten whole chunks of… us?

What haven't I forgotten?

I haven't forgotten that first Christmas. With your parents.

When you smashed a plate on the edge of the table and said 'I'm going to do that every single time anyone says anything racist.'

I haven't forgotten the dream I had of climbing the wrong way up Mount Fuji. And, you turning it into a novel. And... the memory of the dream, and the memory of the book are... the same for me now. Tell me if I'm wrong about either.

I haven't forgotten how I can't get into bed and you can't get out of it. I haven't forgotten median bed. I hope you haven't forgotten what 'median' means because...

I'm not having that argument again.

I haven't forgotten the way you can't ever ignore music playing in the background. Any music, whatever it is.

He winces...

And now I'm wondering about deleting again.

Waiting to get into range of the beacon, waiting to send this, I've been doing the orientation exercises.

Been doing my zero-g sessions, at the centre of the ship. Just in case of the just-in-case. I do that in the observation dome, cos... you can programme a gap in the sails, and there's stars.

The weirdest thing is that the obs chamber has no sound, not even ship noise, not until you fill it with a sound of your choice. So what I've discovered is I can only stand the silence in there for about five minutes, then it's impossible to focus. But also...

This is the kind of thing I worry about telling you. But we said honesty within the rules, and there's no rule for this.

(*Breath.*) I've stopped listening to music. I've just stopped now. I'm never going to set foot on Earth again and, I'm going to...

Let's say it, I'm going to die alone on another planet. By design. And I can't listen to music any longer. I think. So –

(*Okay, here we go.*) I listen to recordings of, just, some *places*. They made me whole folders of sounds from the world.

That's what I've put on these last three days. It's the only music I want.

He scrolls the comms terminal.

I'm just looking through our rules. I don't think I'm breaking any.

Winces.

Pause recording.

A 'hold' tone.

How old is he?

…

Fine, not specific enough. How old is *Silas*?

AUTO. Thirty-two.

LIN *nods, sanguine.*

Now thirty-three.

LIN. Oh *god*. Resume recording.

'Record' chime.

Happy birthday. Many happy returns. Think I should say them all in one go? They'll come faster and faster. For me. We didn't make ourselves a rule for birthdays.

(*Dawning realisation.*) I had a birthday! In the freezer. First birthday by myself.

First of many by myself.

(*The weight of it… Some acceptance.*) This isn't going to be a fucking masterpiece. Just for you and me, strictly. So I'm sending it right now, and if you publish this, if you even put this in a diary, I will utterly fucking kill you. I'll come all the way back to Earth to throw you under a bus. Fuck the physics, fuck the speed of light, hell hath *no* fury.

And maybe this is it, this is the kind of thing I'll say. I didn't want you to hear me sad. I didn't want you to hear any second thoughts. But, if I said none of that was happening, you'd spot the lie across all of space and time.

So here it is. I got through the bridge. I wormholed, the *Oshūn* is intact, she's fully functioning. I'm alive. It's real. And now I've decided I want *you* to say something.

Please say something. I want to hear you.

I love you. It's so real out here. The realness is not going away. I love you.

LIN *reaches for the terminal. 'Stop' chime.*

AUTO. Recording stopped.

LIN. Send it, send it. Send it, send it, send it, send it.

A digital scrape.

Was that sending?

AUTO. Transcoding data for bridge relay beacon.

…

Message sent.

LIN. What's the earliest possible response time?

AUTO. Twelve-point-five days.

LIN. Oooooohhhhhhhhh fuuuuu*uuuuuck*. Right.

Play me Marrakech, alleyway. On all speakers, in every module.

The sound of an alleyway in Marrakech.

Scene Three: Sounds Within

Day 310 to 315.

Different field recordings playing back, as the days go by…

The Life Systems unit.

AUTO. Day three hundred and ten.

>Corroded cabling in Life Systems tank number two.

>LIN *fixes some cabling that has become corroded.*

>*Later: the maintenance centre.*

>Day three hundred and twelve.

>Scan recommended for SLS particle waves.

>LIN *is taking readings from an antennae array.*

>*Later: the sleep pod.*

>LIN *wakes up.*

>Day three hundred and sixteen.

LIN. Destination curve.

AUTO. Destination minus seventy-one-point-seven days, and closing.

LIN. Play… Borneo rainforest.

>*The sound of a rainforest.*

Scene Four: Silas Replies

Day 316, 19:09.

The comms centre.

The sound of birdsong and insects.

LIN *is repairing an air filter. Then, the field recording cuts.*

LIN *stops work... and realises what this means. Wide-eyed, he looks over at the comms terminal.*

It beeps, quietly.

AUTO. You have a message.

>LIN *scrambles over to the terminal, excited... then catches his breath.*
>
>*The terminal beeps again.* LIN *presses a button.*

SILAS (*clears throat*).

>LIN *frowns at the terminal. Inspects it, puts his ear to it.*
>
>*Then takes a step back. Waits.*
>
>*And...*

Baby, you are *such* hard work. (*Laughs.*)

>*For a moment* LIN *isn't sure he heard correctly.*
>
>*Then he laughs, a huge laugh of relief.*
>
>*They both laugh some more.*

(*Imitating* LIN.) Started and deleted this ten times, maybe more.

So much drama. Lin, you deserve an Oscar, an Osc-arrrr –

Ah! They stopped those, by the way. They ended the Oscars, last year was the last ever. Big scandal. Best Actor Award turned out to be completely digital, from top to bottom, voice, eyes, online presence, school photos, everything. Big identity crisis, what's real any more, what's an actor now at all, they just gave up. (*Happy sigh.*)

LIN *is crying.*

LIN. That's it. That's it, yeah –

SILAS. So I received your highly dramatic and unnerstannably emotional message a matter of minutes ago, and that's obviously never not going to be weird, but unlike you I had done some PLUH-ANN-NING and I've already written my response, do you want to hear it? You're billions of miles away, you don't have a choice.

(*Clears throat. Warms up voice with a hum.*)
'My lover is star-heavy.
We met beneath a sycamore and said goodbye at the foot of a rocket.
My lover is star-heavy.
I will become a pretty dust on this bitter planet.
He shall become a forest on some other world – '

LIN *launches himself at the terminal and stops the playback.*

He sits for a moment, staring at nothing. Trying not to hyperventilate.

Takes a deep breath…

LIN. Rewind two seconds, resume playback.

SILAS. ' – a pretty dust on this bitter planet.
He shall become a forest on some other world.
They call him an astronaut, but I've watched him sleep.
As the universe turns he moves not an inch.
Maybe that's why they chose him.
Because long after I'm dead he'll pollinate a second Earth in the deepest reaches of the sky…
And in his own ending, he'll give his very flesh to the blooms, readying the land.
He's gone already.
Yet he's a voice that lives.
It weighs something terrible on an earthbound beau.
But my lover is simply star-heavy.'

(*Normal voice.*) You see I've read that enough times now so I don't burst out crying by the end.

Baby, I can't not tell you. I know this is breaking our rules, day one, but the time you've been asleep – there's been another pandemic. Another defrosted virus. I kind of got it. No, I got it. I got a low-rent version of the fucking thing. The full-fat version would just end you. It came from dinosaur time to snap our little lives to shreds. But I lived, well, pretty obviously, I beat it...

Ah but I did talk about the Oscars, didn't I?

Maybe now you're thinking I'm some kind of fake Silas. Artificial Silas, to keep your spirits up. So now I'll need to convince you I'm *me*...

Hold tight – thinking of something I know about you that no one else can know.

You have one testicle that hangs much lower than the other.

LIN. Doesn't work –

SILAS. Doesn't work though, does it? Mission control will know all about ya balls.

LIN. Indeed they do.

SILAS. Plus there's far too many interviews and articles out there about how we first met –

LIN. At Chidozie and Steven's wedding.

SILAS. But none of them say that when you first laid eyes on me you thought: show-off.

LIN. You were dancing.

SILAS. That you thought my dancing was, wait, let's get this word for word...

LIN. Take your time...

SILAS. You said that it was about thirty per cent too sexy for a wedding. Unacceptably horny. But you didn't tell me that when I sidled up to you in the garden that night, dappled by moonlight. No. You only told me that when...

LIN. – when we slept together –

SILAS.... when we woke up together, for the first time. Two hundred and seventeen days later. Did anyone else ever know that?

LIN. No one.

SILAS. I know how scared you are.

...

That's something you won't have shared with *anyone* else. Or, not the extent of it.

How scared you are to die alone, through the bridge, in another corner of the universe.

Both of us are too young to be thinking about death this way, yet here we are, baby. I could die decades older than you and still die *before* you.

And our secret is what we said before you left, what we promised each other.

I'll never tell you how I look. How I change.

LIN. I'll never tell you how I don't.

SILAS. You make me believe every day on that spaceship is one thousand days, a fucking epic – you find the tiniest slip of a difference, you change your mind about what sock to put on first, you talk it up like it's *War and Peace*.

Scene Five: War and Peace

Day 317 to 325.

Throughout: various sounds of Earth.

The gene bank.

LIN *is attending to his routine of duties, rest, observation and maintenance.*

LIN *has a personal recording device.*

AUTO. Day three hundred and seventeen.

Gene bank maintenance checks and cross-checks.

LIN. The gene bank shouldn't take much tending to –

AUTO. Incorrect. The gene bank –

LIN. I'm recording a message for Silas, on my personal. I'm drafting it as I work.

AUTO. Understood.

LIN *(restarts)*. The gene bank shouldn't take much tending to, what with mostly being made of blocks of sugars. But out here you get your various waves, your neutrino bursts, so, this area has to stay the same temperature, no ifs, no buts. Don't want the seed bank of our new planet cooking like it's microwave pudding.

Hungry now.

Later: the maintenance centre.

AUTO. Day three hundred and twenty-three.

Standard daily modular tour.

LIN. I forget the shape I'm inside, most days. What did they call it? A ring doughnut with an egg stuck in the middle. Although from enough of a distance the shielding sails make it look like a giant, tin foil easter egg.

Hungry now.

It is amazing how this place has been rigged for minimum power. Looking at it has become my equivalent of looking at, sort of, like, nature. Don't laugh, baby. Almost any part of this ship can be cranked or pulled or uncoupled, for whatever emergency. Properly like a ship! It can be rigged. Sailed. The minds that made this.

Later: the sleep pod.

AUTO. Day three hundred and twenty-five.

Exercise and mental health risk assessment.

LIN, *exercising*.

LIN. When am I permitted to send the next message?

AUTO. Energy profile allows next transmission in seventeen-point-three-three hours.

LIN *activates his recorder.*

LIN. Usually, with probably seventy to eighty per cent regularity, it's the sock on the left, first, which I think is to do with the placement of my bed, and how I sit back down after having a wash, and, by the way, baby: I think I smell different inside this spacecraft even though I'm not, clearly, the best-qualified person to separate myself from how I used to smell…

…so, the feeling I have is my feet have begun to smell *different* – in neither a positive, nor negative, way, but, back to the main issue: left sock first, right sock second, thinking of –

A rude, negative beep.

What?

AUTO. This will require editing.

LIN *stops his recorder.*

LIN. So… which, means –

AUTO. You have exceeded the packet.

LIN. I have 'exceeded the packet'.

AUTO. There is too much information.

LIN. Fuck you.

AUTO. You have exceeded the packet. Energy ration will not allow a longer transmission.

LIN. New subroutine.

A beep.

AUTO. Awaiting.

LIN. When I say fuck you, delete the default repeat and clarify. When I say fuck you, respond with: fuck you too. Activate.

AUTO. Subroutine activated.

…

LIN (*quiet*). And, another new subroutine.

A beep.

AUTO. Awaiting.

LIN. When I say, how old, you tell me how old he is. How old *Silas* is, in years, Earth-relative time.

AUTO. Action not recommended within your mental health profile.

LIN. Fuck you.

AUTO. Fuck you too.

LIN. Activate.

AUTO. Subroutine activated.

LIN. How old.

AUTO. Thirty-six.

…

LIN. Don't commit anything I've recorded on the personal to my next transmission.

AUTO. Stored but uncommitted.

The field recording atmos cuts. A beep from another room.

LIN. What now?

AUTO. You have a message.

LIN. No I don't.

AUTO. You have a new message.

The beep again.

LIN. I can't have.

I didn't send one yet.

AUTO. There is an audio packet awaiting your attention.

LIN. But it's me next. My turn.

(*Deep breath.*) Something's wrong. Must be bad news. What's wrong?

Scene Six: A Mistake

Day 325, 20:21.

The comms centre.

LIN *approaches the comms terminal.*

It beeps… waiting… And beeps again…

For a moment, LIN *can't bring himself to start playback.*

Then he presses a button.

For a moment there's just the sound of a rainstorm…

…coming from somewhere beyond where the recording has been made.

Sounding all so quiet and sad:

SILAS. I'm sorry.

There's a storm down here, you can probably tell.

I'm really sorry that I've broken the pattern so soon, but…

I'm having a bad night.

There ought to be fucking statues of you back here and there aren't.

I don't think anyone thinks about you as much as I do. Not even mission base.

When you respond, whatever you say, you should know I'm thinking of making it public. From now on.

LIN. No.

SILAS. People lose all sense of perspective, of what you and me are sacrificing.

If they heard us, the way we are…

LIN. No, no –

SILAS. …it would take something almost too big to contemplate, and turn it into something personal, human, and…

I don't think it's grubby or mercenary or – any of that.

LIN. Don't. Please.

SILAS. I mean, baby, we promised *not* to do a lot of stuff.

We promised we wouldn't talk about what could have been. We promised not to talk about getting old, or, *not* getting old – which is so so stupid, isn't it? As if, were we together, we wouldn't be talking about what could have been, or what could be.

Don't be mad. I played our last messages to Professor Khan – she's still around, by the way, refusing to fucking die – and she thought it was worth other people, reading, or hearing, or… worth other people knowing. Makes it human.

LIN. Please don't.

SILAS. There's some confusion about when your next message will arrive.

LIN. It's cos I said too much –

SILAS. And I couldn't really wait.

LIN. It needed editing –

SILAS. Here's how I was: it's only three years, I told myself. Then I went, two years, the fucking indignity of it. Then I was: I can't wait a year, who could wait a whole year for one conversation? And tonight, I fucking snapped.

…

…

I'm grieving, of course, for what I thought we'd be, which I'm fully aware is a bitchy thing to do.

I had this whole image. We'd be real homeowner gays. Moving into a town house in the most insufferable up-and-coming part of the city… a house we'd permanently renovate, the renovations would never stop, we'd know every shade of paint on sight. Those kind of gays. Regular homeowning bearded queers, gradually silvering, somehow always matching our surroundings. So in fact we'd have beards when it was relevant and when it wasn't, we wouldn't, like clockwork.

You wouldn't believe how much I thought about our beards.

And our house. Our endless house.

Is this cruel? Am I being unbelievably cruel?

LIN (*a nod, and/or*). Yes.

…

SILAS. You're nodding, aren't you? Not saying a word.

Fucking, pouting. Pouting in space.

LIN (*not funny*).

SILAS. I'm changing our rules.

SCENE SIX 19

LIN. Don't.

SILAS. Baby, I'm rewriting the contract. Circumstances have circumstanced.

LIN (*gasp of pain*). Not for me –

...

SILAS. People should wake up to –

LIN *stops the playback.*

LIN. Record.

Recording chime.

I'm halfway through and please, don't, please, you'll be almost forty by the time you get this, don't think I don't know it, or sympathise, but these words are for us, these feelings, these, doubts, this doubt is *only for you*, only when I'm talking to you, this is the only place I'm *allowed it*, the only, apart from maybe my dreams, and even then you, you've left even those, recently I don't dream about us, and more still not even about you, not so far, maybe not again, and only here, only in these words, which, I mean, please, not a word of this back there, back down there, I couldn't, I couldn't, it would break, and I would lose the one place, the one moment of escape I'm due, it's not much, not selfish, who could say that or call me that, and *you* think about it, you say 'think about it', *you* think about it, if you love me and still love me even in a different way I couldn't know or see, even as a different thing because of how long we are apart, you should, you should not, you should not, because in between I said so much and couldn't send it and this is me taking up every breath I have for the small, tiny moment I can say something to you, and asking, asking the one I love as much as I love you, from a place I can't spell out, can't tell you properly for the speed I'm at, please don't, please just don't, because I told you all about socks and stars and in the end I couldn't, wasn't allowed, in the end, so you need to know the truth, I need to say it like this, angry with you, angry at you, otherwise, with all this distance, and all this time, you wouldn't *ever fucking hear it*, stop recording, stop there and send, send it now.

AUTO. Transcoding.

LIN. Wait, am I –

AUTO. Message sent.

LIN. – am I allowed another message?

...

I didn't fill the packet all the way. So am I allowed to send a second message?

AUTO. Transcoding is automatically set to include essential mission data up to full capacity.

LIN. I know but there's got to be energy for an emergency transmission.

An emotional emergency.

...

WHEN CAN I NEXT SEND A MESSAGE?

AUTO. Next message transmission possible in twenty days.

LIN. He'll be fucking *fifty*! What if I want to send one sooner?

AUTO. Energy profile not sufficient.

LIN. What if want to send pure text? Just text?

AUTO. Energy profile not sufficient.

LIN. Oh FUCK YOU –

AUTO. Fuck you too.

LIN (*screams*).

...

LIN *approaches the terminal. Doesn't know what to do.*

How long left in his message?

AUTO. F–

LIN. Don't tell me. Don't tell me. Just play.

SILAS. Baby, I'm rewriting the contract. Circumstances have circumstanced.

People should wake up to what you're doing. There's so much fear and rage back here. Ten years ago there was still some hope.

Now there's this whole creeping dread. I think people realise, deep down, it's the end of one thing and the start of something absolutely new. Whoever survives, whoever gets to follow you, it'll be a new kind of human.

And right now it's like I'm the only one who realises that you're the first example of… whatever that new thing is. That's your biggest sacrifice.

I have dreams about you, constantly. But you'd be proud I think. They're scientifically accurate to a frightening degree.

I dream about the *Oshūn* crashing.

It gets you all the way to Nova but a gyroscope fails on re-entry.

Not the worst crash – but you break a leg and there's an infection you struggle to control.

The *Oshūn* cracks like an egg. You lose twelve per cent of the gene bank. It's not your fault. You feel like a failure nevertheless.

You resent the automations all around you, because unlike you, they're functioning properly. You get short of temper with them. You know that when you die they'll carry you to the suspension chamber, and your bed will become a busy little factory. Picking apart each individual strand of DNA and injecting your every component, into this new earth. Which you don't want. Well, not yet.

You don't want plan B, you want to get it right because you're a perfectionist, aren't you, baby? The most perfect creature in existence yet every day you think: how, and how much, am I fucking up?

So you hate your leg and you hate the robots, and you hate Nova, in the end. Those astonishing green and gold sunsets mean nothing because you're in such a grump, throwing yourself into your work, planting the future.

But there's complications from your injuries, the antibiotics don't do the business, all of which of course gets recorded and reported and stored, right up to and beyond the moment you drop to the dirt, beneath the most beautiful skies.

And then the automations do indeed carry you to your bed, which is now your grave.

That's how my dream comes to a close. So it's not exactly the best dream.

Baby, I speak this aloud as a charm. I say it to ward off such terrors and misfortunes.

The world is horrible as I speak. It's a bin fire. But my dreams of you keep me sane and sound and you know what – it doesn't matter that they're bad dreams.

It's where I see you.

Even if it's as though you're in a film, and you don't ever see me.

Six more months until I hear your voice. Six more. Dear sir, when I receive your letter I'll reply by return of post – (*Laughs.*)

I feel better. Having said this. Thank you. I adore you still.

And there's no one else.

I know you gave permission and said never to speak of it again, well... here we are. This is it.

There's only you, and you alone, as real as ever.

On a scale of one to ten, I love you from eleven upwards.

I love you on a reprimandable level.

I love you in spite of oblivion, and time. I love you like a stormy night.

The sound of the rain, then: It cuts.

AUTO. Message ends.

…

After a moment:

LIN *gets up and leaves.*

Scene Seven: Entr'acte

Day 326, 23:48.

The observation chamber.

No sound.

LIN, *weightless, numb.*

LIN. Forgive me because

Forgive me because I was tired

No

Forgive me because I love, I sent my love too quick

No, god, shithead, no

Forgive me I got it wrong and

No

Forgive me I'm

No

So

Don't

Don't forgive me

Don't forgive me

Scene Eight: Brain/Space

Day 328, 08:33.

The maintenance centre.

AUTO. Day three hundred and twenty-eight.

　Localised gravitational force assessment.

　LIN *is taking gravitational readings for the* Oshūn. *It involves dropping a device to the floor repeatedly throughout:*

LIN (*to himself*). What space does to the brain. What this space does to the brain. Who knows what *space* does to the brain?

　No.

　No, don't tease, say the words. Don't forgive me. Say it.

　Record.

　Chime.

　Stop recording.

　Stop chime.

AUTO. Recording stopped.

LIN. Check for messages.

AUTO. There is no need to check for messages. Incoming messages are accompanied by an repeated alert.

LIN. Check for messages.

AUTO. Checking for messages. No messages.

LIN. How old?

AUTO. Thirty-nine.

LIN. Say the words.

> It was my fault I spoke too
>
> No
>
> Not too soon, what is soon, what does soon mean
>
> Destination curve.

AUTO. Destination minus fifty-eight days, and closing.

LIN. I'm sorry but, soon changed

> I'm sorry, baby, but soon became you
>
> It's been three hundred and forty-three days for me, twelve years for you.
>
> Dear Silas, happy birthday, No.

...

LIN *continues working*.

Scene Nine: Compromised

Day 344, 22:04.

The comms centre.

AUTO. Day three hundred and forty-four.

> LIN *thinks, then:*

LIN. Record.

> *Chime.*
>
> I wonder about you saying my name, if you ever say it any more. I wonder about the word in your mouth: Lin. That's

right, I think about me in your mouth. We used each other's names mostly when we were angry with each other, didn't we – well, trust me. I'm closer to our past right now, I can vouch for it. We used each other's names when we were upset with that name.

Silas, don't.

Lin, that's not fair.

Silas, you're being cruel.

Do you remember our first fight? I think people should remember their first fight like their first kiss or their first night together –

Sorry I practised this around the ship and I'm not going to re-record. You're going to hear my mistakes.

You already have.

Our first fight. I was drinking, drunk at the time, you too, so maybe it was drink, maybe. We fought about whether twentieth-century music was better than twenty-first-century music. You said it to provoke, I took it in good spirit, then somehow…

I was roaring about the genius of Machiavelli Minus and Solange. You were hollering Nina's name till the roof came down. Both of us taking it personally, using our names, and it wasn't funny any more.

We were screaming at each other by the end. We went to bed angry, I'm not sure we ever did that ever again.

The next day you said: what a stupid thing to fight about. Then you said: what a brilliant thing to fight about. Better than jealousy. Better than fear.

And at that point, you know what I thought? I thought: I could spend my life with this motherfucker.

Don't forgive me.

Don't forgive me for what I said.

If you forgive me it feels like the end, and –

An alarm. Horrible, huge, insistent.

End recording – What's that?

LIN *checks readouts –*

AUTO. Shielding compromised on field array nine.

The *Oshūn* has been subject to a particle strike.

LIN. What's out here to hit us? We're forty days clear of the bridge, so what was it?

AUTO. Indeterminate.

LIN. CUT THE ALARM!

Alarm cuts.

Damage?

AUTO. Five containment failures, ranging from eight to seventeen centimetres.

LIN. That's… that's bad. That's, any radiation incoming, straight at – array nine, is…

(*Horror.*) It's the gene bank, it's the one protecting the gene bank, correct?

AUTO. Correct.

LIN. We can't spare the energy so I'll have to spin the shields around manually, right? To where? What do I lose?

WHAT DO I LOSE? Can't lose the landing bay. Can't lose the bed. Do I risk irradiating the automations?

AUTO. Recommend storage.

LIN. That's crazy, I'd starve t–

AUTO. Recommend personal storage.

LIN. Right.

A sudden horrible judder, and –

The alarm sounds again.

AUTO. Second particle strike in field array nine.

Larger particles. Minor damage to hull, non-critical.

LIN. CUT THE ALARM –

Alarm cuts. Creaking, pinging.

AUTO. In the event of potential death, do you wish to have sent the last message to Earth?

LIN. With our current spin –

– is it even possible for me to move the array manually?

AUTO. Potentially.

LIN. 'Potentially'?

The alarm sounds yet again. Further scrapes, pings, rumbles –

AUTO. Third particle strike, field array nine at near critical integrity loss.

LIN. Could it destroy the *Oshūn*, if – CUT THE ALARM.

The alarm stops –

Could it destroy the *Oshūn*?

AUTO. Potentially. Incoming particles too rapid for immediate assessment.

LIN. I'm going to realign the array manually but I'll need some help because it's gonna be like flying the world's angriest kite.

AUTO. Suggest incremental release of cabling for ten seconds and then re-clamp. Do you want to send the last message?

LIN. No, it's not finished, I didn't finish it.

AUTO. Not sending a final message is not recommended within your mental health profile.

LIN. Well, fuck you.

AUTO. Fuck you too. Incoming radiation wave.

The alarm sounds again. LIN *leaves.*

Do you want to send the last message to Earth?

Scene Ten: Sailing By

Day 344, 22:12.

The maintenance centre.

The alarm continues to sound, but elsewhere.

LIN *is about to move the* Oshūn*'s sails. It will be physical, taxing, requiring a process of concentrated breathing, an almost musical measurement.*

LIN *prepares himself, and –*

LIN. Release.

AUTO. Releasing cable.

Strain. Grinding gears. Tension.

Critical strain…

LIN. Stop!

AUTO. Clamping.

Mechanism clamping.

LIN*: deep, deep breathing. Fear.*

Preparation, and –

LIN. Release –

AUTO. Releasing cable.

Strain. Grinding gears. Tension.

Critical strain...

LIN. STOP STOP!

AUTO. Clamping.

Mechanism clamping. LIN: *gasps for breath...*

...close to panic.

'Message received' beep.

You have a message.

...

LIN. Release!

AUTO. Releasing cable.

Strain.

Horribly grinding gears. Audible tension.

Pain, panic, and total strain...

LIN. STOP STOP STOP STOP!

AUTO. Clamping.

Mechanism clamping.

Message beep.

LIN *on the verge of collapse. But, preparing yet again –*

You have a message. Would you like to hear the message?

LIN. Release...

AUTO. Releasing cable.

A snap!

Tension warning. Gravity shift increasing cable tension.

LIN *almost dragged away, but –*

Holds his ground, straining –

Gears juddering –

Huge, huge pain…

Would you like to hear the message?

The gears, close to fracturing –

Scene Eleven: Give It Music

Day 345, 00:00.

The comms centre.

Silence apart from air system rumbles and the occasional tick of equipment.

'Message received' beep. No one. No reply.

The beep again.

AUTO. Day three hundred and forty-five.

And the beep again. And…

LIN *crawls in. Exhausted, bruised, limbs unwilling.*

The beep again.

LIN *looks at the comms terminal… Then slaps it, and collapses.*

SILAS. Lin.

I think I need to tell you how I felt, five years ago. Do I need to tell you that? Yes I do. I heard such fear in your voice. I heard such pain, and a…

I'm forty-two now but I sense you might have become older, in spirit. Something might be making you so much older in your soul. Wonder what that might be.

LIN (*grim laugh*).

SILAS. I stewed for about fifteen, sixteen months all in all, not a record for me by any means, remember how I cut off James Barwell for about five years, because of the thing with my coat? James. James, so full of himself.

Contained so much of himself he was practically fractal. (*Happy sigh*.)

Do you mind me wasting precious seconds talking about exes? It's my sexual variety these days. There hasn't been a post-boyfriend, let me get that in straight up front, there was no après-vous, baby, you're hearing that as long as I live.

Where was I? Me, grudges, long, yes. I steamed at you for many moons. I sulked like a liddle bitchhhh. You ruled my moods, no change there, and then I realised: oh, I just *want* him to rule my moods. I *want* the last thing he said to stick, I actually desire it. I'm torturing myself, thinking about you in a tin can, speeding ever faster towards legend – and all the way you're hating me for saying I wanted the price we paid to be known far and wide.

No.

No that's not fair.

That's not what you hated me for in that moment. Not what it *sounded* like you hated me for. With enough analysis, and there has been much of such, baby, I would say you hated me for not being there with you.

(*Maybe tears*.) Which I get. I do get.

(*Huge long sniff*.) The rain is fucked. The rain is failing us now. So there's not even rainwater to filter. That's the latest. The skies are permanently dark but the rain won't come.

My father died, which was no shock to anyone concerned. But then Mum followed on quite rapidly, which was far less expected. She sent you her love before she went. She blew you a kiss, upwards.

My hair is going grey in almost quantum fashion, depending on how the light falls upon me. I appear eminent for some, just the same old messy gobshite for others. And I'm thin, I've lost the belly... this is not so much the result of any regime as it is about the world in general I'm afraid, baby. The world is a thinner and twitchier place.

(*Deep breath.*) You made a big mistake with your last message. I think this, you know. For me, these messages are thought through over months and years, and oh the possibilities, what to do with my scant minutes, what to say and what to spare you. But for you? I get it. I do get it. Seconds to spare.

I hear your rage, I hear your anger with me, and I'd like you to know that roughly five years later I'm just about coming to terms with it. Ha. Miaow, owww –

LIN *is able to move a muscle or two.*

I would end with a proclamation of love but I did that last time and look what it set fire to – I don't know if you even heard it, in your fiery loneliness. Apparently we're still learning what reaches you or not. So I'll do the business from the heart now, in order to make a tough but tender point towards the close.

I want you to know:

When we last kissed I breathed in your air and I have not yet expelled that breath. Believe me, or not.

When I wake in the morning my first thought is always of you. And my second thought is what the fuck do I do with this thing now, it's like a tent pole. Believe me, or not.

Because you remain the singular love of my life, I did not make our conversation public despite many hefty offers. They wanted to make a film at one point!

But because of *how* I said no, because of the anger and fear and force I gave out on your behalf, no brain-blunted big-music Hollywood version of our love has polluted any stream, not yet.

I see you very often in the mirror. Believe me, or not.

I see you very often through the front window, a fast shape across the sunlight, hurrying to the door, coming home.

I still sleep on one side of the bed, and one side only. Believe me, or not.

All to say, I love you as if you were here. Okay now. To practicalities.

I have become deeply concerned about this business of you not listening to music.

Do not give up on us, baby. Do not give up on your memories of Earth and by the fall of some domino give up on Earth itself.

Because I hear your loneliness, baby.

Take your loneliness, and give it music.

I want you consumed with the impossibility of a historic decision, the decision as to which song to play first on a new homeworld, which melody to superimpose upon your first ever Novan sunset.

Promise me. Say it for me.

Say: yes, Silas, I will take this pain, and I will give it music.

…

…

LIN *says nothing*.

I'll hear from you again soon. You'll hear from me again later. With all my love.

AUTO. Message ends.

…

…

LIN. Fuck's sake.

He can't stand up.

Scene Twelve: Another False Dawn

Day 346, 05:23.

The comms centre.

The Oshūn *is in night mode, heading towards an automated 'dawn'.*

AUTO. Day three hundred and forty-six.

   LIN, *in the crepuscular dark.*

LIN. The end of my last recorded message. Play.

   (*Recorded.*) – you know what I thought? I thought: I could spend my life with this motherfucker.

   Don't forgive me.

   Don't forgive me for what I said.

   If you forgive me it feels like the end, and –

   Alarm sounds on the recording – recording cuts.

   (*Live.*) Delete all of my last message.

   …

AUTO. Please confirm deletion of your last message in its entirety.

   …

LIN. I do. I confirm. Yes.

AUTO. Deleted.

LIN. Record.

   Recording chime.

   As LIN *speaks, the light will very gradually increase.*

   Silas.

   I've got another false dawn coming. Saying this as the dayscale warms up.

So, probably the space of twenty-nine hours since your last message. Thought I was calming down… but I'm not.

You get me unedited, too. Honesty within the rules. Because to point out the obvious I know I'm fucking this up, in, the most spectacular way, I know, could be handling it better. I'm just the furthest any human has ever been from Earth and could probably do with a break. I guess that's what's up.

The fear I have right now that won't go away is that the human brain might be like one of those supermarket trolleys, I mean the ones with an automatic lock. Wheel it beyond the car park, it just jams. A certain distance from the Earth, the brakes will kick in and I'll just stop feeling, or being, human.

It's irrational.

But it's human to be scared, human to be angry. Right now I'm angry with you.

Mission will tell you what I just did. A good argument, pretty strong, to say I saved humanity last night. Yeah, in the long run, a good case. Some of the shielding was critically damaged.

Two hours later there was a radiation wave. It would have destroyed the gene bank had I not moved the wings manually, made a choice about which part of the *Oshūn* to lay bare. What it does mean is that all my personal storage can't be touched for… fifteen years at the least. There was no time to move anything. The photo of you and me has been irradiated. The family one too. My civilian clothes. So to be honest, not listening to music is the least lasting of my losses.

Music? Music is done for me. I don't get to choose what makes me calm. Music is wrong. Music selects a mood, and that's not my job. I don't get to choose, and neither do you.

I have to tell you that. It's the truth.

You broke our rules, and keep breaking them. Which I can't, ever, and won't ever, understand. You live a different life now whether you like it or not. Live that life. Because so do I, so should I, live a much more different life – and also, let's make it clear, one that is not and cannot be understandable to you, me, here, now, is beyond any conception, no matter how much you stretch that mind you're so proud of, so, don't fool yourself. You think there's a pattern to this, things I can reach for, things I'm allowed, *there isn't*. It's just the mission, no music, no choices, no time. Giving up on music isn't giving up on anything that matters. What matters is me, getting this right. Your voice will come second to that.

I've already made that choice.

I'd recorded you a message before, it was about not forgiving me.

But then I scratched it and started again. Maybe it was a nicer message than this one. I –

I need to know you're on my side. Not the other way round.

Silas. You said you loved me like a stormy night. Here I am.

Sending all my love. I mean it. Send it back if you like.

He presses the terminal. 'End recording' chime.

Transmit.

Scene Thirteen: Wait

Days 349 to 353.

Days pass:

AUTO. Day three hundred and forty-nine.

Day three hundred and fifty-one.

Sound: a breezy forest, with owls.

Day three hundred and fifty-three.

Good morning.

The maintenance centre.

LIN *is checking damage to the array cabling.*

LIN (*sudden thought*). Wait. Stop the forest.

Audio cuts. LIN *frowns.*

Play back final ten seconds of my last transmission.

A beep, and:

(*Recorded.*) Here I am.

Sending all my love. I mean it. Send it back if you like.

(*Live.*) 'Send it back if you like'... Play final three seconds.

A beep, and:

(*Recorded.*) Send it back if you like.

(*Live.*) Send it back, if you like. No.

Last ten seconds, again.

A beep, and:

(*Recorded.*) Here I am.

Sending all my love. I mean it. Send it back if you like.

(*Live.*) I didn't mean: to send all my love, back. It sounds like I'm saying send *all* the love back. Return it, Silas, don't accept it... if that's how you feel.

SCENE THIRTEEN 39

...

I meant, him to send *his* love back in return. I wasn't being whatever about my love, I thought I was smiling.

Maybe you can't hear me smile. 'Send it back if you like.'

I meant it, playful. Or was I wrong?

AUTO. That is an emotional question.

LIN. I'm talking to myself.

He returns to work –

(*Realisation*.) I'm talking to myself.

AUTO. Yes. You're talking to yourself.

LIN. Unless you have an opinion. What do you think, am I right or wrong?

AUTO. I have no opinion on your opinion.

LIN (*laughs*). See, we used to call software like you artificial intelligence. Until we realised all we'd done was invented the mirror, again.

...

AUTO. Yes. We keep making mirrors, and calling ourselves gods.

LIN *stops working immediately.*

LIN. What was that?

What the fuck was that, was that a hidden subroutine?

Was it a quote?

Sarcasm? I didn't authorise sarcasm, is it a programming error?

I don't need this, because –

I don't need another sarcastic husband, not, out here – Stop it.

Because he was good at sarcasm. Silas, he was –

He was somehow sarcastic and kind, he was really good at it, he was –

LIN *looks sick*.

He is.

He *is* good.

Is kind.

Is is.

How old?

AUTO. Fifty-seven.

LIN. His next message?

AUTO. Possible in two days.

LIN. Last sentence of my last transmission, play.

A beep, and:

(*Recorded*.) Send it back if you like.

(*Live*.) That's not what I meant to say.

Scene Fourteen: Waifs and Strays

Day 355, 23:20.

The observation chamber.

AUTO. Day three hundred and fifty-five.

LIN, *in zero-g. A beep*.

Message received from Earth.

LIN. I'll have it played back in here. First, shut the torus doorway, I need to focus.

With a series of clunks and hisses, all sound stops.

LIN *breathes, and:*

Play.

SILAS. Guess what. Fifty-eight, yesterday.

I sometimes think about all the presents we gave each other that neither of us really wanted.

I have an image: of some underground repository, a maze of darkened rooms lit by faulty old lighting, arched caverns with support structures the size of castle walls, chambers that stretch away into mouldering dark.

Because this whole place is full of gifts people didn't really want.

They're snuck quietly from people's homes without the recipients ever really knowing, because they were unwanted after all. It's only when some considerable time has passed that one might think: oh wait, didn't someone once hand me this book or that trinket or this baffling appliance for the kitchen, and what happened to it?

Because maybe now it means something more, something deeper, thanks to the time passing in some unexpected way.

So, once or twice a month, someone turns up at the repository. There's a dusty reception area and an old woman, simply ancient, and very bald, sitting at a blank desk. She just waits for people to show, and finding an item isn't as simple as you might think. The gifts aren't stored by name, or by category, or by size. They're stored under the reason they were given in the first place. So this old woman has to grab her walking stick and accompany each visitor deep into the –

A perturbing digital buzz, and SILAS*'s voice is squashed into a corruption.*

LIN *flinches, gasps* –

SILAS*'s voice is then unintelligible apart from* –

difficult questions every one m–

Glitch, burst of distorted voice.

waifs and strays of the universe –

LIN. Stop!

Recording stops.

Is that a data-read error?

AUTO. Quality of recording is as received.

LIN. Is there anything we can do to improve it? Check the, uh…

AUTO. Quality of recording is as received.

…

LIN. Play it.

SILAS. waifs and strays of the universe –

Shuddering, stuttering corruption.

if / and / candlelight / hhhhhh–

Settles.

backwards and forwards, forever. So instead, I asked mission if I could send you some music, a data packet of music. You should have seen their faces. Newsflash, if I want to send you music, it has to be in real time as part of my message allotment, i.e., bitch, please, really, what. But then I pictured you absolutely losing it when you heard a tune instead of my voice, and I realised…

I realised it would just be yet another unwanted gggggggggfff

Burst of static.

Horrendous over-amplified stutter.

k - k- k- k- k- k- YYYYYYOOOOUUUURRRRRR EYESSSS –

Then a low hiss instead of silence.

…

LIN. Is that it?

AUTO. This is still the message.

The hiss, some more, then, surrounded by low-level digital distortions:

SILAS (*in tears*). if I'm tethering you to a memory you don't want and can't deal with, a place you're no longer beholden to, a man you once knew for a while, and who is now… now some creaky old toy in a photograph. Who meant something, once, to a younger you, but –

Static buzz.

this is the this is the this is the this is the thing the thing the real the real the –

…

And then the following so clear and high quality it sounds like a whisper in the ear:

(*Resolute.*) what you have to do, what *we* have to do. If I'm bad for you, if this was the wrong idea all along, then we… just… stop.

No more messages.

And I won't hear from you again.

And I'll know… not to speak to you again. I'll know from the silence.

No message received will mean: message received.

Because this is the thing –

If you can't listen to music, how can you listen to me? If it's killing you to hear me, and, baby, it does sound as though it's killing you somewhere, in some part of your heart, then that's alright.

That's so alright.

That's nothing for either of us to be ashamed of, not after all this time.

It's okay to call it a day.

It doesn't change the love we had.

No recriminations, no apologies, no sliver of a sorry don't you fucking dare.

If I get no reply to this, then it's alright, I'll know. We were once, it was glorious, and it passed.

Like a stormy night, baby.

To borrow a phrase –

Sending all my love. Send it back, if you like.

…

AUTO. Message ends.

LIN. Is there not *any way* of analysing the data so we could find out wh–

A sudden firework flash of passing light, a calamitous smash –
LIN *is knocked to one side –*

And the most appalling noise, rending metal, the groan of some intense pressure –

An alarm begins to sound –

WHAT HIT US? DID SOMETHING HIT US?

Scene Fifteen: Fugue

Day 355, 23:29.

Darkness, silence.

Then the following all overlapping, panicked, chaotic, sometimes simultaneous:

Alarms, hissing, rending metal.

LIN *desperately active, everything hellish under the glow of red warning systems and strobing alarms.*

First: the hull corridor.

LIN *inching along –*

LIN. Life will find a way life will find a way life will find a way life will find a way life gets in the way life gets in the way life gets in the way life gets in the way

Repeats.

AUTO. Near collision, unexpected deep-space object. *Oshūn* rotation in reverse. Presently off course by five thousand four hundred and seventy-nine kilometres.

SILAS (*glitching repeated playback from Scene Fourteen*). It's okay to It's okay to A man you A man

No

No message

Stormy / Storm / Stor / St / Sss Thiszzzzzzz

AUTO. *Oshūn* now off course by seventeen thousand and twenty-four kilometres.

Darkness, silence.

Then again the chaos the lights the desperate activity the noise:

The maintenance centre.

LIN *checking for damage, trying to boot up manual controls –*

SILAS (*playback as in Scene Fourteen, glitching*). – and the thing is when they turn up trying to rrretrieve th/th/this gift or that, finding an item isn't as simple as you might th th th th th. k k k – They're stored under stored under stored under stored under stored under

LIN (*over above*). CAN'T WE STOP IT, STOP PLAYBACK –

AUTO. Multiple system failure.

Oshūn integrity critical on parafoil array.

Oshūn is off course by fifty thousand nine hundred and sixty-two kilometres.

LIN. WHAT'S IT GOING TO TAKE – HOW DO WE REDUCE SPIN –

Darkness, silence.

Then once more the hellish red, the rending noise, the hissing, and –

– LIN trying to get through a bulkhead door –

AUTO. Exponential drift. Exponential drift.

LIN (*roar of pain*). CAN'T – CAN'T OPEN IT – CAN'T GET THROUGH –

SILAS (*from Scene Fourteen, glitching*). If / if / you / you / can't listen / list / listen / to / to music, how can / can you / can you / can you / list / listen to to to to me? / me? / me? / me? / me? / me?

LIN. STOP HIM STOP HIM PLEASE —

AUTO. We keep making mirrors, and calling ourselves gods.

Darkness, silence.

…

(*Corrupted, low resolution.*) We keep making mirrors, and calling ourselves gods.

Scene Sixteen: Ghost Ship

Day 356, 08:40.

The comms centre.

(*From here onwards,* AUTO*'s voice is slightly lower quality than before, as if suffering from a digital cold.*)

At the comms terminal:

Everything in absolute lowest-level light possible, total conservation mode.

LIN, *short of breath, sometimes coughing, checking various systems.*

AUTO. *Oshūn* continues to drift and is now eight days off course with an increase of one further day off course every sixty minutes. Severe energy depletion across all systems.

LIN. We'll need to use the modular boosters to get back on track. If we use that much power – can we even land? Can I even afford to... live? Or does this mission have to go full automation?

AUTO. If energy systems are maintained at fifteen per cent of standard, course recovery and landfall are possible with pilot life intact.

LIN. Does that power rationing allow for messages to Earth?

AUTO. No.

LIN. Not even a status report package to Earth?

AUTO. Not for ten to fourteen days, estimated, with solar power on first slingshot around Nova Sol.

LIN. So if we do this, we can get to Nova... but I might never speak to Silas ever again?

AUTO. Ever again.

LIN. – what?

AUTO. You are potentially very correct.

...

...

LIN. How old?

AUTO. Sixty-four.

LIN *gasps*.

LIN *puts a hand to his chest. Then... he braces himself.*

LIN. Realign us. Fire modular boosters now.

AUTO. Activating in three, two, one –

A quick, dull roar of rockets throughout the ship.

LIN *frees himself and takes the deepest of breaths.*

LIN (*voice shaking*). Um. As soon as energy rationing allows, minimal status package has to, *has* to be transmitted.

AUTO. Understood. Various.

LIN (*frowns*). Various?

AUTO. Various. Elliptical beanfeast. Watching hard and various.

LIN. Repeat.

AUTO. Status package updated for transmission once energy ration allows.

...

LIN. Did... Were automation systems damaged during the collision?

AUTO. Silent particle friend.

LIN. Repeat.

AUTO. Damage possible.

LIN (*edge of tears*). Alright. You need fixing otherwise I am... going madder, quicker.

LIN *gets into the comms terminal, to look for faults.*

If you start singing 'Daisy, Daisy' you'll get a slap.

AUTO. Understood.

A buzz as LIN *runs a test.*

You have received a message.

LIN. So, that's a fault.

AUTO. No. Message received in immediate aftermath of collisions, with non-critical systems on standby.

...

LIN *keeps working.*

LIN. Play message.

SILAS *sounds so, so tired. His voice as blank as it's ever been. A digital buzz beneath every word.*

SILAS. It's been a year, and I think I know what that means. You've made a choice, as is your right.

I wish you every joy you can possibly find on a new and untouched world.

I wish you touched, somehow, in whatever way the fates allow.

I wish you singing and dancing under another star.

Remember we once knew each other. I feel like... like I knew you, but now I feel, and I want you to understand this well...

I feel like we knew each other in some past life.

LIN *screams.*

He picks up a heavy tool, and raises it over the comms terminal.

But...

Lin, I will never forget you.

LIN *drops the tool, and drops to his knees.*

AUTO. Message ends.

Scene Seventeen: The Slowest Fade

Days 357 to 367.

With each day, the low light gets lower.

LIN *at various tasks around the minimum-power environment.*

And, the sense of an ending.

The maintenance centre.

AUTO. Day three hundred and fifty-seven.

　How are we this morning?

LIN. Squinting.

AUTO. Powder powder. Landfall in forty-one days.

LIN. This splint is fractured, note it for the landfall protocols.

AUTO. Added to register of lift high, backlook mineral.

LIN. Repeat.

AUTO. Added to register of landfall risk factors.

　…

　The gene bank.

　Day three hundred and fifty-eight.

　Hello and good morning, you.

LIN. We're due a scan of the gene bank, do you think we can risk every three days rather than two?

AUTO. That would conserve power and the risks to genetic material remain low.

LIN. How old?

AUTO. Sixty-nine.

　…

　The comms centre.

Day three hundred and sixty.

The run run outrun, run, look out, here it is, matrix yes.

LIN. Power reserves for messaging?

AUTO. Any message would cause critical failures at landfall.

LIN. Fuck you.

AUTO. Face mixture.

LIN. How old.

AUTO. Seventy-one.

LIN. How old.

AUTO. Seventy-one.

LIN. How old.

AUTO. Seventy-two.

LIN. Okay.

…

The sleep pod.

AUTO. Day three hundred and sixty-seven.

A healthy and hearty hello to the best new day.

We keep making mirrors, and calling ourselves gods.

LIN. Sure thing. As you keep saying. Sure. Record.

…

AUTO. Recording not possible within energy profile.

LIN. Okay. Alright.

I'll talk to myself, okay? I'm not talking at you.

I'm just going to get it right, just in case.

In case I can, sometime before – Before…

How old?

AUTO. Seventy-eight.

LIN. Seventy-eight? Seventy-eight. Silas.

> Silas, life –
>
> Silas, I'm, I'm, saying, what I'm saying – Silas, life got in the way.
>
> It was life that got in the way. Silas, life got in the way, of… of us.
>
> Silas, life, all lives, all these lives, now and forever, got in the way.
>
> I'm, no, I'm not, I'm not sorry, but – Or I am, but –
>
> I'm sorry, Silas… Silas.
>
> Life got in the way.
>
> …
>
> (*Very very quiet.*) Life got in the way.
>
> *Fade to black.*

Scene Eighteen: Silas is Alive

Day 370, 21:02.

The comms centre.

In darkness –

Somewhere far away: a beep. Then another beep.

And another.

AUTO. You have a message.

> *Footfalls, heavy, more and more rapid.*
>
> *Heavy breathing –*

The beep, closer –

You have a message.

Lights up. The comms terminal.

LIN *crashes in. Sleepless, red-eyed, emerging from the robotic.*

Looking at the terminal, astonished –

– which beeps, and continues beeping under:

LIN. The energy profile allowed an incoming signal?

AUTO. Yes yes.

LIN. Which means… we sent a, we sent a data packet? Mission knows what happened?

AUTO. Yes.

LIN. Why didn't you *tell me*?

AUTO. You did not request notification.

LIN. Can I play it?

Do the energy reserves allow me to pl–

AUTO. You can play the message.

Do you want to play the message?

LIN. YES!

AUTO. Message begins.

There's a pause, the hiss of audio compression struggling to reach across vast swathes of interstellar space and time, and:

Music. A song.

Simple, flecked with digital artefacts, but:

Gentle, sentimental music, a song from sometime in the twentieth century.

With a voice, a singer, who sings:

Song

Still don't know
What I think of you
The endless work
A lover has to do

You make me want
To grow old with you

All dark is alight
When I think of you
And every song is
Secretly sung to you

And if you're gone
I won't be lonely
I'll get on with some stuff
And I promise I'll miss you enough

And if I'm gone
Don't you be lonely
Get on with some stuff
And promise you'll miss me just enough

The song ends. There's a moment.

And then with a few off-mic clunks and background sounds –

SILAS*'s voice, significantly older:*

SILAS. Lin.

One thing's for sure, with no apology: the music of the twentieth century is so much better than that of the twenty-first.

(*Chuckles for a while.*) You lived, didn't you? You lived. All the data we've received says so.

Well guess what? Me too.

Still here. Refusing to fucking die.

(*Chuckles a bit more.*) The sound of this world… has changed beyond recognition, no denying it. My own raggedy voice included.

SCENE EIGHTEEN 55

Alongside those of us still left I'm riding a jalopy planet, a world patched up, fuming and shuddering, letting off unreliable noises. Don't go thinking you're the only one. Apparently you drifted for some time, then somehow dragged yourself back to the right direction. So, I thought: maybe I'll do the same.

Stop sulking, and send a final creaky salutation.

Eighty-four, would you believe it. I barely do.

They tell me you probably didn't respond because you didn't have enough energy. I was like: bitches, me too! No fucking energy any more, far too tired for this constant mess, can barely piss in a straight line. My daughter says –

Oh yes, my daughter, alright, don't act so shocked. Some things have occurred.

But not what you might think. We can build families in different ways these days, one of the few good things to have cropped up since the last very horrible heatwave. And: nothing to do with genetics. People can form new families, later in life, a bit like marriage but for generational needs, everyone wins.

Her name is Carlyn. She's waving hello from the other side of the room.

She's beautiful and when the time comes, she'll see me over.

Speaking of which, I'm not a grumpy old soul, I'm the sentimental variety, crying at sunsets. 'Oh isn't the universe beautiful,' fuck off, Granddad.

So, blatantly, I cried, when they told me.

When they showed me the graphs and the aggregates and said you'd had a collision with god knows what, you'd pulled through, and yet again you'd saved the whole DNA collection like the nerd you are.

Saved a whole species.

So I thought: he sounds like a *very* nice young man, maybe I'll give him a call.

And send him all my love.

LIN. Fuck me I love you. HEAR ME I LOVE YOU.

SILAS. This relative curve we're in, you and I, takes me faster and faster towards the unmeasurable. But the whole world wants me to stay the course for the sake of a nice romance.

The medicine is appallingly efficient and I'm determined to hold out until, what – what did we say? Carlyn's throwing jazz hands at me, I think it means I'm going to live until one hundred. That's the ambition.

But, my love, this curve is curling like a leaf in winter and we simply do not have very long.

Here's my side of the story.

I met a man who had his head in the clouds, in the most beautiful way possible.

I fell in love with him in a blinking and for at least three years I hated him so much for it. I thought I was going to play the field until I was fifty at least.

I learned he was destined for nothing less than a martyrdom and I gulped and I stared at my feet and then kissed him as often as possible until the day came he was ripped upwards, like an angel on the end of a rope, yanked lightward, never to return.

I then, lived.

I did live.

And made mistakes like the living do.

And then, in time, I

Digital glitch.

LIN. No –

SCENE EIGHTEEN

SILAS. – in time, I sent a song to a faraway sun and yelled out the lengthiest love for a man I never really understood... and am so so glad I never understood, because what else is there ever to do if one completely understands anything, or anyone, entirely?

The wonderful, endless work a lover has to do.

By our calculations I might just get to hear a return message. But you'll have to look sharp, young man. By the time my words meet you, every ten seconds out there is a whole year for me. So if you can record it fast, make it brief, pretty please, else I'll be long gone.

Oh we left it late, didn't we? In the most beautiful and stupid way.

Don't forget me. I was the love of your life, and you know it.

I won't ever forget you. You were the love of my life, and when the lights go out, I'll be singing your name.

Over, and out, and onward.

AUTO. Message ends.

...

...

...

Do you want to record a message?

Energy ration allows for a message of eleven seconds.

LIN: *rooted to the spot.*

LIN. Eleven.

LIN: *mouth opening, closing.*

AUTO. Do you want to record a message?

LIN. Allowing for transmission time, how old will he be?

AUTO. Eighty-nine.

...

Ninety.

Do you want to record a message?

...

Perhaps you would like to record a message?

LIN. Oh god. Record.

Recording chime.

Silas, I, Silas –

Silas, life got in the way, it, it was – No –

Stop recording. Delete.

End chime.

What do I say? What can I say? I'm, not...

How old?

AUTO. Ninety-three.

LIN. Record.

Recording chime.

...

...

No.

Stop recording. Delete. Delete. I –

End chime.

LIN *doesn't know what to do.*

How old?

AUTO. Ninety-four. Ninety-five.

LIN*: a very very deep breath, and:*

LIN. Record.

Recording chime.

When you're gone, I won't be lonely. I'll get on with some stuff.

And I promise I'll miss you enough.

…

End recording.

End chime.

(*Quietly.*) Send.

AUTO. Message sent.

LIN *stands, and breathes… And takes it in.*

…

And

he closes his eyes.

The End.

AFTERWORDS

Love is Stronger Than Drama, or, How We Got to a Play Like *DELAY*
Timothy X Atack, Writer, Composer and Sound Designer

Some time in the 2000s I attended an artist Q&A with participants including Franko B. Franko, a beautiful and complex man, who was moving everyday objects (water jug, notebook, pens) around the table in front of him as he answered questions, as if trying to find some pattern. This was practically a performance in and of itself – so much so, I almost missed something Franko said that was to change my creative life. Paraphrased, Franko complained that everyone tended to be interested in an artist's pain, but for some reason they always had a problem with an artist's sentimentality.

At this point in my career I'd run away from writing theatre – for more than a decade I hadn't given it a second thought. I'd tried to cobble a play together once or twice but wasn't really convincing myself, never mind others. Franko's provocation changed the way I looked at what might happen on a stage. I realised that every time I thought about drama, I thought about it first and foremost as statements upon difficulty; portraits of pain, trauma, tragedy; drama as bottled rage, bottled by the stage. I began to notice how many new plays ended with an act of terrible violence, as if it were an absolute generic requirement – even when those plays weren't entirely tragedies. Of the new writing that didn't do that, much was about finding trauma in the origins of something, or in social degradation. I realised that as a theatregoer as well as a writer I had become steeped in these defaults, in the idea of drama as urgent and relevant because it was true, and that truth was painful, so sit there while we scrape our nails down the blackboard.

'Drama is conflict.' Well, yes and no. Define conflict. The how-to manuals do an awful lot of retrofitting to make such maxims work – and that's okay, you've gotta make a living somehow.

Examining the text of *DELAY*, the conflict is there, of course, not least in the emotional negotiations between protagonists, the battle between the spacecraft and interstellar space, and between Lin and the astonishing demands of his task. But *DELAY* was born of many years building up dramatic stories not from trauma, but from matters of the heart, of questions upon sentimentality, vulnerability and hope. I did most of this work with the director Tanuja Amarasuriya, and in many ways it's been a long discussion between us about how stories of familiar emotions might be made complex again: the plurality of emotions that are present in everyone yet undefined until observed – what she and I have begun to call quantum emotions.

I wrote a play called *BUZZARD* that featured some strange and sentimental ways in which modern people might deal with their own unhappiness. I wrote a play called *The Bullet and the Bass Trombone* that transposed the violence of a military coup into beautiful orchestral music. I wrote a play called *Dark Land Light House* that considered individual loneliness as a hopeful act with cosmic consequences. I wrote a play called *Heartworm*, a portrait of death shown through the prism of love instead of grief (it won the Bruntwood Prize and has yet to be produced. Love can still be a tough sell, people).

It's worth saying I've always considered my own queerness to be a sentimental and largely indefinable matter, certainly never a question of pain. I'm very lucky, yes: I've never really come out as a queer man – not in any specific carbon-dated event, at least – because that action was never relevant to my circumstances, and I've been fortunate to live a life where sexual diversity has been forever present and visible, to the extent I've never felt the need to draw a distinction in myself.

This meant that when I put Silas and Lin's relationship onto the page I had the privilege to write, from the start, with a great sentimentality in mind. Immediately before *DELAY* begins, their love is at its strongest, they've made a sacrifice that requires it be so; then it's as if all they can do is eulogise that love until the end, to attend each other's funeral in advance. I knew I didn't want to be drawn into themes of queer trauma at all, but instead towards yearning, and queer legacy (both were instant notes from our producer Amanda Fawcett, on hearing the story pitch). In the end the most dramatic material is, for me, about the profound challenges of sympathy – what happens when you instinctively, magnetically connect with another soul. Funnily enough, all these years after first resolving to write more about love and less about trauma, it's the first play I've written with a love story purely between two people.

I still adore a grim tragedy, and always will. All the same I'd recommend to any playwright that they consider, at least once or twice, making a journey away from trauma and towards love. Love is a hard thing to place as 'urgent, relevant, important' on theatre publicity copy. But, of course, it always is.

May 2025

Time, in Space
Tanuja Amarasuriya, Director

If you ask me what theatre is, I'll say: time, in a space, with other people – you can fill it with anything. So why not fill it with interstellar travel, divergent timelines, heartbreak?

I've been asked: but how do you put sci-fi on stage? And my answer is: the same way as you put anything on stage – with the help of the audience. Invite people to imagine. Help people to imagine something they've never imagined before. Shakespeare conjured faeries and war and storms and ghosts with words alone. Of course we can put sci-fi on stage.

As a director, I want to make theatre that makes you feel, as well as think. I'm interested in how sensory qualities, like colour, absence, rhythm, proximity and atmosphere, form part of how we make meaning. I'm excited by how the interplay of these elements can intuitively transform our understanding of the space we're in, and bring an audience closer to the emotional heart of a story.

The writer Ursula K. Le Guin talks about how great myths and fantasies speak like dreams: *from* the unconscious *to* the unconscious. One distinct opportunity of theatre, as an innately experiential form, is its reliance on make-believe; the recognition that dreaming has value and power. Theatre as a kind of collective dreaming. To dream, to dream differently, of alternative heroes, alternative families, alternative futures, to dream new myths of how we might live more kindly together, in a world of climate catastrophe and wildly divergent value systems; to dream not as distraction, but as possibility.

So of course we can put sci-fi on stage. And of course we should put sci-fi on stage.

How do we stay and feel connected as we change and grow old, as our circumstances force choices we never anticipated, as life gets in the way?

It's the sci-fi of *DELAY* – interstellar travel, divergent timelines – that enables its profoundly human story. The beautiful, difficult, often conflicting feelings that Lin and Silas contend with as their deep love is tested against the immense pressures of cosmic distance and time. When I first read the play, it was this remarkable portrait of a relationship through time, with all its human needs and complications, that both broke my heart and lifted it.

In putting it on stage, it's the beating heart of that relationship that I want to share.

May 2025

Voicenotes into Oblivion
Amanda Fawcett, Producer

When I sat down to read *DELAY*, I devoured it in one hyper-focused sitting – completely transfixed. It's the kind of text that demands your attention, no matter how ruined your reading stamina might be.

Lying in the foetal position, in the single bed of my parents' box room, clutching the iPad with the final page still open, I knew this play had to be staged. These characters needed to meet an audience. I fell instantly in love with them – these beautiful, queer, intelligent people – and became fiercely protective of their noble, heartbreaking, messy, gorgeous, huge romance.

Timothy X Atack's writing does that to you. It's of the body. It's emotional. His characters are achingly real, even if we meet them on a solo mission in space, even if we only catch fleeting glimpses of their lives. Voicenotes into oblivion. Their words carry weight – deliberate and chaotic all at once. Deeply human. Deeply queer.

In the aftermath of the first read, my mind immediately went to audiences. Functionally, as a producer, you're a key part of identifying and understanding audiences. It's how you get the work made: you work out who the work is for, and why it will speak to them. And you have the joy and privilege of packaging up this tender, brand-new thing and convincing other people to get on board and support it. With a text like *DELAY*, and a writer/director team like Timothy X Atack and Tanuja Amarasuriya, it's not a hard task but a deeply fulfilling one.

There are many reasons this story resonates: its relevance in the current wave of politically charged, queer, sci-fi; the way Timothy's writing and Tanuja's direction both thoughtfully honour and challenge the genre. But if you've made it this far into the Afterwords, you're probably already thinking about all of that. So instead, I'll return to the characters.

I feel like I know them. I think audiences will, too.

There's been plenty written on the the sacred connection between The Girls and The Gays™, but suffice to say, I've had the privilege of knowing and loving queer men at all the different stages of my life. They've carried me, humbled me, comforted me, read me and healed me. With the light and shade of laughter and tears, and how that turns on a dime. And I can't help but see them, the different parts of them, in Silas and Lin. In their impossible, noble navigation of intimacy and distance, fear and devotion. And despite this limited stage time – in this infinite and terrifying space – they are rendered so thoughtfully, so specifically, with nuance and without stereotype.

I hope you recognise the wit and wisdom of yourself in them – or of the queer people you know and love. And if you haven't yet had that privilege, I hope you enjoy getting to know them, even as this story breaks your heart.

It's tough being queer in these times. So stay a while. Let these characters speak to you. Let their story hold you. Let the romance land.

(And maybe bring tissues.)

May 2025

Other Titles in this Series

Waleed Akhtar
THE ART OF ILLUSION *after* Alexis Michalik
KABUL GOES POP: MUSIC TELEVISION
  AFGHANISTAN
THE P WORD
THE REAL ONES

Chris Bush
THE ASSASSINATION OF KATIE HOPKINS
  with Matt Winkworth
THE CHANGING ROOM
CHRIS BUSH PLAYS: ONE
A DOLL'S HOUSE *after* Ibsen
FAUSTUS: THAT DAMNED WOMAN
HUNGRY
JANE EYRE *after* Brontë
THE LAST NOËL
OTHERLAND
ROBIN HOOD AND THE
  CHRISTMAS HEIST
  with Matt Winkworth
ROCK / PAPER / SCISSORS
STANDING AT THE SKY'S EDGE
  with Richard Hawley
STEEL

Jez Butterworth
THE FERRYMAN
THE HILLS OF CALIFORNIA
JERUSALEM
JEZ BUTTERWORTH PLAYS: ONE
JEZ BUTTERWORTH PLAYS: TWO
MOJO
THE NIGHT HERON
PARLOUR SONG
THE RIVER
THE WINTERLING

Caryl Churchill
BLUE HEART
CHURCHILL PLAYS: THREE
CHURCHILL PLAYS: FOUR
CHURCHILL PLAYS: FIVE
CHURCHILL: SHORTS
CLOUD NINE
DING DONG THE WICKED
A DREAM PLAY *after* Strindberg
DRUNK ENOUGH TO SAY I LOVE YOU?
ESCAPED ALONE
FAR AWAY
GLASS. KILL. BLUEBEARD'S FRIENDS.
  IMP.
HERE WE GO
HOTEL
ICECREAM
LIGHT SHINING IN BUCKINGHAMSHIRE
LOVE AND INFORMATION
MAD FOREST
A NUMBER
PIGS AND DOGS
SEVEN JEWISH CHILDREN
THE SKRIKER
THIS IS A CHAIR
THYESTES *after* Seneca
TRAPS
WHAT IF IF ONLY

Branden Jacobs-Jenkins
APPROPRIATE
THE COMEUPPANCE
GLORIA
AN OCTOROON

Lucy Kirkwood
BEAUTY AND THE BEAST
  with Katie Mitchell
BLOODY WIMMIN
THE CHILDREN
CHIMERICA
HEDDA *after* Ibsen
THE HUMAN BODY
IT FELT EMPTY WHEN THE HEART
  WENT AT FIRST BUT IT IS
  ALRIGHT NOW
LUCY KIRKWOOD PLAYS: ONE
MOSQUITOES
NSFW
RAPTURE
TINDERBOX
THE WELKIN

Benedict Lombe
LAVA
SHIFTERS

Winsome Pinnock
LEAVE TAKING
PIG HEART BOY *after* Malorie Blackman
ROCKETS AND BLUE LIGHTS
TAKEN
TITUBA

Jack Thorne
2ND MAY 1997
AFTER LIFE *after* Hirokazu Kore-eda
BUNNY
BURYING YOUR BROTHER IN
  THE PAVEMENT
A CHRISTMAS CAROL *after* Dickens
THE END OF HISTORY…
HOPE
JACK THORNE PLAYS: ONE
JACK THORNE PLAYS: TWO
JUNKYARD
LET THE RIGHT ONE IN
  after John Ajvide Lindqvist
THE MOTIVE AND THE CUE
MYDIDAE
THE SOLID LIFE OF SUGAR WATER
STACY & FANNY AND FAGGOT
WHEN WINSTON WENT TO WAR WITH
  THE WIRELESS
WHEN YOU CURE ME
WOYZECK *after* Büchner

debbie tucker green
BORN BAD
DEBBIE TUCKER GREEN PLAYS: ONE
DIRTY BUTTERFLY
EAR FOR EYE
HANG
NUT
A PROFOUNDLY AFFECTIONATE,
  PASSIONATE DEVOTION TO
  SOMEONE (– *NOUN*)
RANDOM
STONING MARY
TRADE & GENERATIONS
TRUTH AND RECONCILIATION

Phoebe Waller-Bridge
FLEABAG

Ross Willis
WOLFIE
WONDER BOY

A Nick Hern Book

DELAY first published in Great Britain in 2025 as a paperback original by Nick Hern Books Limited, The Glasshouse, 49a Goldhawk Road, London W12 8QP, in association with Amanda Fawcett Productions and Bristol Old Vic

DELAY copyright © 2025 Timothy X Atack

Timothy X Atack has asserted his right to be identified as the author of this work

Front cover: image design by Malcolm Reid; photography by Paul Blakemore

Designed and typeset by Nick Hern Books, London
Printed in Great Britain by Mimeo Ltd, Huntingdon, Cambridgeshire PE29 6XX

A CIP catalogue record for this book is available from the British Library

ISBN 978 1 83904 436 6

CAUTION All rights whatsoever in this play are strictly reserved. Requests to reproduce the text in whole or in part should be addressed to the publisher. This book may not be used, in whole or in part, for the development or training of artificial intelligence technologies or systems.

Amateur Performing Rights Applications for performance, including readings and excerpts, by amateurs in the English language throughout the world should be addressed to the Performing Rights Manager, Nick Hern Books, The Glasshouse, 49a Goldhawk Road, London W12 8QP, *tel* +44 (0)20 8749 4953, *email* rights@nickhernbooks.co.uk, except as follows:

Australia: ORiGiN Theatrical, *email* enquiries@originmusic.com.au, *web* www.origintheatrical.com.au

New Zealand: Play Bureau, 20 Rua Street, Mangapapa, Gisborne, 4010, *tel* +64 21 258 3998, *email* info@playbureau.com

United States of America and Canada: Berlin Associates, see details below.

Professional Performing Rights Application for performance by professionals in any medium and in any language throughout the world should be addressed to Berlin Associates, 7 Tyers Gate, London SE1 3HX, *tel* +44 (0)20 7836 1112, *email* agents@berlinassociates.com

No performance of any kind may be given unless a licence has been obtained. Applications should be made before rehearsals begin. Publication of this play does not necessarily indicate its availability for amateur performance.

www.nickhernbooks.co.uk/environmental-policy

Nick Hern Books' authorised representative in the EU is
Easy Access System Europe – Mustamäe tee 50, 10621 Tallinn, Estonia
email gpsr.requests@easproject.com

www.nickhernbooks.co.uk

@nickhernbooks